Golf

G°lf

LIFE ON THE LINKS

Ariel Books

•

Andrews and McMeel
Kansas City

ISBN: 0-8362-1092-1
Library of Congress Catalog Card Number: 95-80759

$5.95 U.S.A. / $8.50 Canada

Introduction

Golf is a simple game, or so it appears at first glance: using as few strokes as possible, hit a small white ball into a cup in the grass. As any devotee will tell you, however, golf moves easily from pastime to obsession. From leaving work early to fibbing to their spouses, golfers will do almost anything in order to hit the greens.

It seems that more is said about golf than about any other sport. Each course has a personality, each player a special quirk or two, and each club or championship a favorite legend. Gathered here are nearly four hundred of the funniest, most sincere, and most outrageous quotations by golf addicts—that is, professional athletes, presidents, movie stars, and comedians.

Golf addiction is spreading: more and more people are opting for life on the links. The challenges and pleasures of the game, the perfectly manicured lawns, and the spectacular views lure players of all ages, from all walks of life, and in all kinds of weather. This is good news, because more time spent on the course—or in the clubhouse—by those who love the game means more witticisms, musings, quips, and tall tales to keep you smiling while you swing that club.

The most exquisitely satisfying act in the world of golf is that of throwing a club. The full backswing, the delayed wrist action, the flowing follow-through, followed by that unique whirring sound, reminiscent only of a passing flock of starlings, are without parallel in sport.

HENRY LONGHURST

At least he can't cheat on his score—because all you have to do is look back down the fairway and count the wounded.

BOB HOPE

The ball's got to stop somewhere. It might as well be at the bottom of the hole.

Lee Trevino

(on putting)

Golf is the hardest game in the world. There's no way you can ever get it. Just when you think you do, the game jumps up and puts you into your place.

BEN CRENSHAW

Nothing goes down slower than a golf handicap.

BOBBY NICHOLS

In golf, humiliations are the essence of the game.

ALISTAIR COOKE

When you play the game for fun, it's fun. When you play it for a living, it's a game of sorrows.

GARY PLAYER

On the golf course, a man may be the dogged victim of inexorable fate, be struck down by an appalling stroke of tragedy, become the hero of unbelievable melodrama, or the clown in a side-splitting comedy.

BOBBY JONES

It's a tan like mine. It tells you the player is spending a lot of time out on the fairway and the greens—and not in the trees.

LEE TREVINO

(on the sign of a good golfer)

Here, Eddie, hold the flag while I putt out.

WALTER HAGEN

(to the Prince of Wales)

Thinking
instead of acting
is the No. 1 golf
disease.

SAM SNEAD

My God, he looks like he's beating a chicken.

BYRON NELSON

(on Jack Lemmon's swing)

He plays just like a union man. He negotiates the final score.

BOB HOPE

(on George Meany)

There is no other loser in sport who has shown himself to be as gracious and warm as Nicklaus has shown himself to be.

HERBERT WARREN WIND

(on Jack Nicklaus)

22

I never knew what top golf was like until I turned professional. Then it was too late.

STEVE MELNYK

The only time I talk on a golf course is to my caddie. And then only to complain when he gives me the wrong club.

SEVE BALLESTEROS

Around a clubhouse they'll tell you even God has to practice his putting. In fact, even Nicklaus does.

JIM MURRAY

A perfectly
straight shot
with a big club
is a fluke.

JACK NICKLAUS

Golf is more fun than walking naked in a strange place, but not much.

BUDDY HACKETT

Columbus went around
the world in 1492. That isn't
a lot of strokes when you
consider the course.

LEE TREVINO

Miss a putt for two thousand dollars? Not likely!

WALTER HAGEN

Tiger Woods?
I thought that was a golf course.

SANDY LYLE

(on junior golf star Tiger Woods)

Golf is the only game where the worst player gets the best of it. They obtain more out of it with regard to both exercise and enjoyment. The good player gets worried over the slightest mistake, whereas the poor player makes too many mistakes to worry over them.

DAVID LLOYD GEORGE

If you're going to be a player people will remember, you have to win the Open at St. Andrews.

JACK NICKLAUS

Don't hurry, don't worry. . . .
Be sure to stop and smell
the flowers.

WALTER HAGEN

You swing your best when
you have the fewest things
to think about.

BOBBY JONES

I retired from competition at twenty-eight, the same age as Bobby Jones. The difference was that Jones retired because he beat everybody. I retired because I couldn't beat anybody.

CHARLES PRICE

Serenity is knowing that your
worst shot is still going to
be pretty good.

JOHNNY MILLER

I see some wonderful young players on the tour. But I also see many who will be doing something else for a living before too long.

HARVEY PENICK

That's the trouble with Nick. The only time he opens his mouth is to change feet.

DAVID FEHERTY

(on Nick Faldo)

Caddies are a breed of their own. If you shoot sixty-six, they say, "Man, we shot sixty-six!" But go out and shoot seventy-seven, and they say, "Hell, he shot seventy-seven!"

LEE TREVINO

Isn't it fun to go out on the course and lie in the sun?

BOB HOPE

Golfers are very fond of insisting, and with great justice, that the game is not won by the driver. It is the short game—the approaching and putting—that wins the match. Nevertheless, despite the truth of this, if there were no driving there would be very little golf.

HORACE HUTCHINSON

They are the same people who knock the pyramids because they don't have elevators.

JIM FERREE

(on players who complain about the course at St. Andrews)

Baffling late-life discovery: golfers wear those awful clothes on purpose.

HERB CAEN

He's the biggest thing
in the desert since sand.

BOB HOPE

*(on Arnold Palmer winning the Hope
Classic in Palm Springs five times)*

Golf is typical capitalist lunacy.

GEORGE BERNARD SHAW

Trent Jones must have laid
this one out in a kennel.

BOB ROSBURG

*(on all the doglegs at the Hazeltine,
Minnesota, golf course)*

I don't care to join any club
that's prepared to have me
as a member.

GROUCHO MARX

One of the nice things about the Senior Tour is that we can take a cart and cooler. If your game is not going well, you can always have a picnic.

LEE TREVINO

The truly great things happen when a genius is alone. This is true especially among golfers.

J. R. COULSON

I sure was glad I ran out of holes. I looked down at my hands and arms to see if it was me when I finished with the score.

DON JANUARY

Golf is the only game in which a precise knowledge of the rules can earn one a reputation for bad sportsmanship.

PATRICK CAMPBELL

Golf is assuredly a mystifying game. It would seem that if a person has hit a golf ball correctly a thousand times, he should be able to duplicate the performance at will. But such is certainly not the case.

BOBBY JONES

The winds were blowing
50 mph and gusting to 70.
I hit a par 3 with my hat.

CHI CHI RODRIGUEZ

(on the windy course in Scotland)

The player may experiment about his swing, his grip, his stance. It is only when he begins asking his caddie's advice that he is getting on dangerous ground.

SIR WALTER SIMPSON

Most golfers prepare for disaster. A good golfer prepares for success.

BOB TOSKI

Hagen said that no one remembers who finished second. But they still ask me if I ever think about that putt I missed to win the 1970 Open at St. Andrews. I tell them that sometimes it doesn't cross my mind for a full five minutes.

DOUG SANDERS

When Jack Nicklaus plays well, he wins. When he plays badly, he finishes second. When he plays terribly, he finishes third.

JOHNNY MILLER

All good players have good hands. And I'm afraid you have to be born with them.

DAVE STOCKTON

I play by memory. If somebody tells me to hit the ball 150 yards, I hit it 150 yards.

SAM SNEAD

(on his poor vision)

Beyond the fact that it is a limitless arena for the full play of human nature, there is no sure accounting for golf's fascination. . . . Perhaps it is nothing more than the best game man has ever devised.

HERBERT WARREN WIND

Everyone has his own choking level, a level at which he fails to play his normal golf. As you get more experienced, your choking level rises.

JOHNNY MILLER

Golf is neither a microcosm of nor a metaphor for life. It is a sport, a bloodless sport, if you don't count ulcers.

DICK SCHAAP

There is no movement in the golf swing so difficult that it cannot be made even more difficult by careful study and diligent practice.

THOMAS MULLIGAN

I like going there for golf.
America's one vast golf
course today.

EDWARD, DUKE OF
WINDSOR

You can talk
to a fade but a
hook won't
listen.

LEE TREVINO

Do I ever disagree with him on course strategy? Never— unless he's wrong.

GARY NICKLAUS

(on caddying for his father)

I try to build courses for the
most enjoyment by the
greatest number.

ALISTER MACKENZIE

Man blames fate for other accidents but feels personally responsible for a hole in one.

MARTHA BECKMAN

I feel calm in calm colors.
I don't want people to watch
the way I dress. I want people
to watch the way I play.

SEVE BALLESTEROS

In a team sport, you can go out and make your own breaks. You can make a tackle. You can jump up and block Julius Erving's shot. In golf, you're all alone. Sometimes it's hard. I can't run out and jump on Jack Nicklaus's back.

ANDY NORTH

On the golf course, a man may be the dogged victim of inexorable fate, be struck down by an appalling stroke of tragedy, become the hero of unbelievable melodrama, or the clown in a side-splitting comedy.

ROBERT TYRE JONES

The reason the Road Hole is
the greatest par 4 in the world
is because it's a par 5.

BEN CRENSHAW

*(on the seventeenth hole
at St. Andrews)*

After an abominable round of golf, a man is known to have slit his wrists with a razor blade and, having bandaged them, to have stumbled into the locker room and enquired of his partner, "What time tomorrow?"

ALISTAIR COOKE

When I get out on that green carpet called a fairway, manage to poke the ball right down the middle, my surroundings look like a touch of heaven on earth.

JIMMY DEMARET

The only way of really finding out a man's true character is to play golf with him. In no other walk of life does the cloven hoof so quickly display itself.

P. G. WODEHOUSE

A tolerable day, a tolerable green, a tolerable opponent— they supply, or ought to supply, all that any reasonably constituted human should require in the way of entertainment.

EARL OF BALFOUR

I'd give up golf if I didn't have so many sweaters.

BOB HOPE

I guess there is nothing that will get your mind off everything like golf. I have never been depressed enough to take up the game but they say you get so sore at yourself you forget to hate your enemies.

WILL ROGERS

If I needed advice from my caddie, he'd be hitting the shots and I'd be carrying the bag.

BOBBY JONES

I've lost balls in every hazard and on every course I've tried. But when I lose a ball in the ball washer it's time to take stock.

MILTON GROSS

It could be worse;
I could be allergic to beer.

GREG NORMAN

(on being allergic to grass)

The only time you play great golf is when you are doing everything within your power to lose to your boss.

THOMAS MULLIGAN

Golf is a good walk spoiled.

MARK TWAIN

Have you ever noticed what golf spells backwards?

AL BOLISKA

The three things I love best in the world are sex, golf, and hunting. Far as I can see, I ain't about to stop doing any of 'em.

SAM SNEAD

The more I practice, the luckier I get.

GARY PLAYER

The rest of the field.

ROGER MALTBIE

(when asked what he needed to shoot to win a tournament)

The point is that it doesn't matter if you look like a beast before or after the hit, as long as you look like a beauty at the moment of impact.

SEVE BALLESTEROS

In the golf swing a tiny change can make a huge difference. The natural inclination is to begin to overdo the tiny change that has brought success. So you exaggerate in an effort to improve even more, and soon you are lost and confused again.

HARVEY PENICK

89

She doesn't yell "fore," she yells "liftoff." You don't watch her ball, you track it, an unidentified flying object entering orbit.

JIM MURRAY

(on Laura Davies)

Most people play a fair game of golf—if you watch them.

JOEY ADAMS

A passionately keen golfer died and in due course found himself in Hell. To his delight, however, he immediately came upon a superb golf course. "This is a marvelous surprise, but why is no one playing?"

The reply came: "This is Hell, you know. The problem is that there are no balls."

MICHAEL HOBBS

It's a faithless love, but you hit four good shots and you've started your day right.

DINAH SHORE

Golfers find it a very trying matter to turn at the waist, more particularly if they have a lot of waist to turn.

HARRY VARDON

For the first time I felt like they used to feel when they played with me — Mark hits it so hard and far, I felt totally inadequate.

JACK NICKLAUS

(on Mark Calcavecchia)

He must have no nerves at all.

JACK NICKLAUS

*(on the putting abilities of
Deane Beman)*

I compare the pressure of a golf shot with making an extra point in basketball. The player starts from a full stop, and that rim doesn't move.

HARVEY PENICK

My wife is flying out here
tonight. I haven't seen her in
two weeks and I'm horny,
so that should help.

KEN GREEN

*(on his prospects for the
Canadian Open)*

If you really want to get better
at golf, go back and take it up
at a much earlier age.

THOMAS MULLIGAN

I played golf with a priest the other day. . . . He shot par-par-par-par-par. Finally, I said to him, "Father, if you're playing golf like this you haven't been saving many souls lately."

SAM SNEAD

Golf may be played on
Sunday, not being a game within
view of the law, but being a
form of moral effort.

STEPHEN LEACOCK

I've done as much for golf as Truman Capote has done for sumo wrestling.

BOB HOPE

You have to play golf in Scotland. What else is there to do there? Wear a skirt?

GEORGE LOW

Baseball players quit playing and they take up golf. Basketball players quit, take up golf. Football players quit, take up golf. What are we supposed to take up when we quit?

GEORGE ARCHER

He struck Gysbert Cornelisz, tavern keeper, and Claes Andriesz with a golf club at the house of Steven Jansz for which, together, he forfeits Fl 20.

Court minutes of the Colony of Rensselaerswyck, Albany, 1650

We must always be humble in victory and cocky in losing.

CHI CHI RODRIGUEZ

The better you putt, the bolder you play.

DON JANUARY

To me, he's very boring. He's never in the trees or in the water. He's not the best driver, not the best putter. He's just the best at everything.

FRED COUPLES

(on Nick Faldo)

A professional will tell you the amount of flex you need in the shaft of your club. The more the flex, the more strength you will need to break the thing over your knees.

STEPHEN BAKER

The last time I had this much fun, I was having a root canal.

LARRY ZIEGLER

(on coming in a distant third at the Masters)

When you reflect on the combination of characteristics that golf demands of those who would presume to play it, it is not surprising that golf has never had a truly great player who was not also a person of extraordinary character.

Frank D. "Sandy" Tutam Jr.

Well, sir, I'd recommend the 4:05 train.

HARRY VARDON'S CADDIE

(responding to Vardon's question, "What should I take here?")

There are two things you can learn by stopping your back-swing at the top and checking the position of your hands: how many hands you have, and which one is wearing the glove.

THOMAS MULLIGAN

It's hard not to play up to Jack Nicklaus's standards when you are Jack Nicklaus.

JACK NICKLAUS

Anyone who criticizes a golf course is like a person invited to a house for dinner who, on leaving, tells the host that the food was lousy.

GARY PLAYER

115

He goes after a golf course like a lion at a zebra. He doesn't reason with it. . . . He tries to hold its head under the water until it stops wriggling.

JIM MURRAY

(on Seve Ballesteros)

Victory is everything. You can spend the money but you can never spend the memories.

KEN VENTURI

Some of us worship in churches, some in synagogues, some on golf courses.

ADLAI STEVENSON

The inevitable result of any golf lesson is the instant elimination of the one critical unconscious motion that allowed you to compensate for all your errors.

THOMAS MULLIGAN

I swear Arnold would sign an autograph at a red light. If a guy pulled up to Arnold in a car and asked him for an autograph, Arnold probably would pull over if he could read his lips.

LEE TREVINO

(on Arnold Palmer's nice-guy reputation)

The golfer has more enemies than any other athletes. He has fourteen clubs in his bag, all of them different; eighteen holes to play, all of them different, every week; and all around him are sand, trees, grass, water, wind, and 143 other players. In addition, the game is 50 percent mental, so his biggest enemy is himself.

DAN JENKINS

Take two weeks off and then quit the game.

JIMMY DEMARET

(advice for an unhappy golfer)

To control his own ball, all alone without help or hindrance, the golfer must first and last control himself. At each stroke, the ball becomes a vital extension, an image of one's innermost self.

JOHN STUART MARTIN

Even the men's room has a double dogleg.

DAVE STOCKTON

(on the Poppy Hills course in Pebble Beach, California)

124

The difference between golf
and government is that in golf
you can't improve your lie.

GEORGE DEUKMEJIAN

If your opponent is playing several shots in vain attempts to extricate himself from a bunker, do not stand near him and audibly count his strokes. It would be justifiable homicide if he wound up his pitiable exhibition by applying his niblick to your head.

HARRY VARDON

The average golfer doesn't play golf. He attacks it.

JACKIE BURKE

It's not whether you win or lose—but whether I win or lose.

SANDY LYLE

Golf puts a man's character on the anvil and his richest qualities — patience, poise, restraint — to the flame.

BILLY CASPER

Golf is an expensive way of playing marbles.

G. K. CHESTERTON

Charley hits some good woods — most of them are trees.

GLEN CAMPBELL

(on his friend Charley Pride)

If you drive,
don't drink.
Don't even
putt.

DEAN MARTIN

The hardest shot is a mashie at ninety yards from the green, where the ball has to be played against an oak tree, bounces back into a sand trap, hits a stone, bounces on the green and then rolls into the cup. That shot is so difficult I have only made it once.

ZEPPO MARX

They throw their clubs backwards, and that's wrong. You should always throw a club ahead of you so that you don't have to walk any extra distance to get it.

TOMMY BOLT

(on the antics of modern players)

A golf course is the epitome of all that is purely transitory in the universe, a space not to dwell in, but to get over as quickly as possible.

JEAN GIRAUDOUX

The only place I can find him is on the sports pages.

EDNA HAGEN

(Walter Hagen's wife)

Golf is a better game played downhill.

JACK NICKLAUS

I don't like #4 balls.
And I don't like fives, sixes,
or sevens on my card.

GEORGE ARCHER

(on his superstitions)

I see things written about the golf swing that I can't believe will work except by accident.

HARVEY PENICK

Give me a man with big hands
and big feet and no brains and
I'll make a golfer out of him.

WALTER HAGEN

He hits the ball 130 yards and his jewelry goes 150.

BOB HOPE

(on Sammy Davis Jr.)

I know I'm getting better at golf because I'm hitting fewer spectators.

GERALD FORD

Every hole should be
a difficult par and a
comfortable bogey.

ROBERT TRENT JONES

The person I fear most in the last two rounds is myself.

TOM WATSON

On one hole I'm like Arnold Palmer, and on the next like Lilli Palmer.

SEAN CONNERY

I say this without any
reservations whatsoever:
It is impossible to outplay an
opponent you can't outthink.

LAWSON LITTLE

Give me my books, my golf clubs, and leisure, and I would ask for nothing more.

EARL OF BALFOUR

I never pray on a golf course.
Actually, the Lord answers
my prayers everywhere
except on the course.

BILLY GRAHAM

In baseball you hit your home run over the right-field fence, the left-field fence, the center-field fence. Nobody cares. In golf everything has to go right over second base.

KEN HARRELSON

Oh the dirty little pill
Went rolling down the hill
And rolled right into the bunker
From there to the green
I took thirteen
And then by God I sunk her!

TRADITIONAL

When I want a long ball, I spin my hips faster.

JACK NICKLAUS

This place is like one of those hot-air hand dryers in toilets. It's a great idea and everybody uses it once, but never again. It takes too long.

DAVID FEHERTY

(on a Grand Cypress, Florida, golf course designed by Jack Nicklaus)

A leading difficulty with the average player is that he totally misunderstands what is meant by concentration. He may think he is concentrating hard when he is merely worrying.

ROBERT TRENT JONES

I never wanted to be a
millionaire. I just wanted
to live like one.

WALTER HAGEN

A day spent in a round of strenuous idleness.

WILLIAM WORDSWORTH

Y ou must attain a neurological and biological serenity in chaos. You cannot let yourself be sabotaged by adrenaline.

MAC O'GRADY

(on playing good golf)

Golf and sex are the only
things you can enjoy without
being good at them.

JIMMY DEMARET

I'll take a two-shot penalty, but I'll be damned if I'm going to play the ball where it lies.

ELAINE JOHNSON

(after her tee shot bounced off a tree and landed in her bra)

The man who hates golfers" is what they call me. They couldn't be more wrong. I design holes that are fun to play.

ROBERT TRENT JONES

Golf is a game in which the ball lies poorly and the players well.

ART ROSENBAUM

Whoever plays ball with a club shall be fined twenty shillings or their upper garment.

THE MAGISTRATES OF BRUSSELS

(proclaimed in 1360)

I'm glad we don't have to play in the shade.

BOBBY JONES

(response to being told it was

105 degrees in the shade)

I may be the only golfer never to have broken a single putter, if you don't count the one I twisted into a loop and threw into a bush.

THOMAS BOSWELL

When you're having trouble
and topping the ball, it means
the ground is moving on you.

CHI CHI RODRIGUEZ

If your adversary is a hold or two down, there is no serious cause for alarm in his complaining of a severely sprained wrist, or an acute pain, resembling lumbago, which checks his swing. Should he happen to win the next hole, these symptoms will in all probability become less troublesome.

HORACE HUTCHINSON

I dreamed I made seventeen holes in one, and then on the eighteenth hole I lipped the cup and I was madder than hell.

BEN HOGAN

There are two basic rules which should never be broken. Be subtle. And don't, for God's sake, try to do business with anyone who's having a bad game.

WILLIAM DAVIS

My hands were shaking on
the last putt. The only problem
with that is you never know
which shake is going
to hit the putt.

PATTY SHEEHAN

(on qualifying for the Hall of Fame)

What earthly good is golf? Life is stern and life is earnest. We live in a practical age. All around us we see foreign competition making itself unpleasant. And we spend our time playing golf! What do we get out of it? Is golf any *use*? That's what I'm asking you. Can you name me a single case where devotion to this pestilential pastime has done a man any practical good?

P. G. WODEHOUSE

I'll be playing center for the Bulls before he's on the Tour.

PETER JACOBSEN

(on Michael Jordan's chances as a pro)

It took me seventeen years to get three thousand hits in baseball. I did it in one afternoon on the golf course.

HANK AARON

Whenever I play with him, I usually try to make it a foursome—the president, myself, a paramedic, and a faith healer.

BOB HOPE

(on Gerald Ford)

You have to make corrections in your game a little bit at a time. It's like taking your medicine. A few aspirin will probably cure what ails you, but the whole bottle might just kill you.

HARVEY PENICK

I told him he was one year away from the Tour and next year he'll be two years away.

CHI CHI RODRIGUEZ

Let your hands take it away, laddie, and feel the grass.

Scottish wisdom on the game

I'm the best.
I just haven't
played yet.

MUHAMMAD ALI

(on golf)

It is almost impossible to remember how tragic a place the world is when one is playing golf.

ROBERT LYND

I owe a lot to my parents,
especially my mother
and father.

GREG NORMAN

Hell, it ain't like losing a leg!

BILLY JOE PATTON

(on losing the Masters)

It would have been a hell of a ride.

JACK NICKLAUS

*(on seeing an ant on top of the golf
ball he was about to hit)*

Golf is a game kings and presidents play when they get tired of running countries.

CHARLES PRICE

It's a grind trying to beat sixty-year-old kids out there.

SAM SNEAD

(on his decision to quit the Senior Tour at age seventy-seven)

A good player who is a great putter is a match for any golfer. A great hitter who cannot putt is a match for no one.

BEN SAYERS

More people show up to watch Lee Trevino change shoes than watch me tee off.

ORVILLE MOODY

Swing hard in case you hit it.

DAN MARINO

Golf is golf. You hit the ball,
you go find it. Then you
hit it again.

LON HINKLE

Only one golfer in a thousand grips the club lightly enough.

JOHNNY MILLER

I needed 'em both.

BOB LANIER

(on playing a round with a doctor

and a priest)

Just knock the hell out of it with your right hand.

TOMMY ARMOUR

I went to bed and I was old and washed up. I woke up a rookie. What could be better?

RAYMOND FLOYD

(on making the Senior Tour at fifty)

Of all the golfers in the world I cannot believe that anyone will make a greater impact upon the championships than this very tough, very determined young man. The world is at his feet and he is only twenty-one years of age.

PAT WARD THOMAS

(on Jack Nicklaus)

I hate a hook. It nauseates me.
I could vomit when I see one.
It's like a rattlesnake in
your pocket.

BEN HOGAN

In so many English sports, something flying or running has to be killed or injured; golf calls for no drop of blood from any living creature.

HENRY LEACH

My conscience hurt me. I hate to play golf when I should be out working, so the only thing to do was quit working.

JIM UMBRACHT

former major league pitcher and salesman

Imagine the ball has little legs, and chop them off.

HENRY COTTON

It's so ridiculous to see a golfer with a one-foot putt and everybody is saying "Shhh" and not moving a muscle. Then we allow nineteen-year-old kids to face a game-deciding free throw with seventeen thousand people yelling.

AL McGUIRE

I'm about five inches from being an outstanding golfer. That's the distance my left ear is from my right.

BEN CRENSHAW

Too many golfers grip
the club at address like they
were trying to choke a prairie
coyote to death.

CURT WILSON

Art said he wanted to get more distance. I told him to hit it and run backward.

KEN VENTURI

(at a roast for columnist Art Rosenbaum)

Golf is a game of expletives not deleted.

DR. IRVING A.
GLADSTONE

All tennis
courts look
alike.

BRADFORD DILLMAN

*(on why he likes golf more
than tennis)*

I owe everything to golf.
Where else would a guy with
an IQ like mine make this
much money?

HUBERT GREEN

I played so bad, I got a bad, I got a get-well card from the IRS.

JOHNNY MILLER

It's good sportsmanship to not pick up lost golf balls while they are still rolling.

MARK TWAIN

Absolutely everyone has done it, but there are few people who admit it.

DAVID FEHERTY

(on choking)

When I play my best, I feel I'm playing with my legs and feet.

SAM SNEAD

Golf is an open exhibition of overweening ambition, courage deflated by stupidity, skill soured by a whiff of arrogance.

ALISTAIR COOKE

What other people may find
in poetry, I find in the
flight of a good drive.

ARNOLD PALMER

I ain't got no nerves. Once you walk a six-inch beam thirty floors above the ground, a three-foot putt doesn't scare you none.

WALTER ZEMBRISKI

*golfer and former high-rise
construction worker*

Golfing excellence goes hand in hand with alcohol, as many an open and amateur champion has shown.

HENRY LONGHURST

This is a game of misses.
The guy who misses the best
is going to win.

BEN HOGAN

The golf swing is like sex:
you can't be thinking of the
mechanics of the act while
you're doing it.

DAVE HILL

Never bet with anyone you meet on the first tee who has a deep suntan, a 1-iron in his bag, and squinty eyes.

DAVE MARR

Golf is a hands game.

HENRY COTTON

Now, when I hit one in the water, the fish will know who to send it back to.

BOB HOPE

(on his birthday gift:
ninety balls inscribed with
"Happy Birthday, Bob")

When I look on my life and try to decide out of what I have got most actual pleasure, I have no doubt at all in saying that I have got more out of golf than anything else.

LORD BRABAZON

One thing about golf is you don't know why you play bad and why you play good.

GEORGE ARCHER

That little white ball won't move 'til you hit it, and there's nothing you can do after it's gone.

BABE DIDRIKSON
ZAHARIAS

It is a sport in which the whole American family can participate—fathers and mothers, sons and daughters alike. It offers healthy respite from daily toil, refreshment of body and mind.

DWIGHT EISENHOWER

The best stroked putt in a lifetime does not bring the aesthetic satisfaction of a perfectly hit wood or iron shot. There is nothing to match the whoosh and soar, the almost magical flight of a beautifully hit drive or 5-iron.

AL BARKOW

There are twenty-three million golfers in this country and most of them are bad. I'm just one of them.

GARY MCCORD

Man, the worst thing about
this is I won't be able
to play golf.

CHARLES BARKLEY

(on a shoulder injury)

All I could think of was, "Good, I don't have to putt."

MIKE BLEWETT

(on a hole in one)

Boy, if the phone should ring,

Or anyone come to call,

Whisper that this is spring,

To come again next fall.

Say I have a date on a certain tee

Where my friends the sand traps wait in glee.

U.S. GOLF CLUB SONG

It's a compromise between
what your ego wants you to do,
what experience tells you to do,
and what your nerves let you do.

BRUCE CRAMPTON

(on concentration)

In my opinion, no young
player can develop his or her
game to its highest potential if
he or she rides around the
course in a golf cart.

HARVEY PENICK

He told me he caddied in the same group with me in the Hot Springs Open. That's why I voted for him, because he was a caddie.

TOMMY BOLT

(on Bill Clinton)

If every golfer in the world,
male and female, were laid
end to end, I, for one,
would leave them there.

MARK PARKINSON

president of the
Anti-Golf Society

I just want to be a household word in my own household.

HOWARD TWITTY

(on fame)

To be a champion, you have to find a way to get the ball in the cup on the last day.

TOM WATSON

Baseball reveals character; golf exposes it.

ERNIE BANKS

Well, that lot's full. Let's see if I can park this baby someplace else.

JOANNE CARNER

(on hitting two drives into a parking lot)

What's nice about our tour
is you can't remember your
bad shots.

BOB BRUCE

(on the Senior Tour)

My favorite shots are the practice swing and the conceded putt. The rest can never be mastered.

LORD ROBERTSON

Golf is not a creative game. A creative actor will reach the top of his profession. So will a creative basketball player. But a golfer whose mind is creative won't make it.

CRAIG T. NELSON

I would rather play Hamlet
with no rehearsal than TV golf.

JACK LEMMON

I like the way my wallet feels in them.

JOHNNY MILLER

(on the clothes he endorsed)

St. Andrews never impressed me at all. I wondered how it got such a reputation. The only reason could be on account of its age.

BILL MEHLHORN

A golf ball is like a clock. Always hit it at six o'clock and make it go toward twelve o'clock. But make sure you're in the same time zone.

CHI CHI RODRIGUEZ

If you play poorly one day, forget it.

If you play poorly the next time out, review your fundamentals of grip, stance, aim, and ball position. Most mistakes are made before the club is swung.

If you play poorly for a third time in a row, go see your professional.

HARVEY PENICK

I prefer to take out the dog.

PRINCESS ANNE

(on golf)

No one remembers who came in second.

WALTER HAGEN

Golf is a game whose aim is
to hit a very small ball into an
even smaller hole, with weapons
singularly ill designed for
that purpose.

WINSTON CHURCHILL

I never pray to God to make a putt. I pray to God to help me react good if I miss a putt.

CHI CHI RODRIGUEZ

Golf is played with the arms.

SAM SNEAD

Only on days ending in *y*.

JERRY WEST

(when asked how many days a week he played golf)

Real pressure in golf is
playing for ten dollars when
you've only got five dollars
in your pocket.

LEE TREVINO

My career started slowly and then tapered off.

GARY McCORD

Real golfers don't cry when they line up their fourth putt.

KAREN HURWITZ

I'm not very good with a gun,
but I'm hot with a wedge.

ANNE-MARIE PALLI

(after killing a duck that flew

across the course)

Golf is in the interest of good
health and good manners.
It promotes self-restraint and
affords a chance to play the man
and act the gentleman.

PRESIDENT TAFT

It's a marriage. If I had to choose between my wife and my putter — I'd miss her.

GARY PLAYER

At first a golfer excuses a dismal performance by claiming bad lies. With experience, he covers up with better ones.

P. BROWN

That putt was so good, I could feel the baby applaud.

DONNA HORTON-WHITE

(on making a twenty-five-foot putt while seven months pregnant)

The golfer is never old until he is decrepit. So long as providence allows him the use of two legs active enough to carry him round the green, and of two arms supple enough to take a "half swing," there is no reason why his enjoyment in the game need be seriously diminished.

EARL OF BALFOUR

You need a fantastic memory in this game to remember the great shots and a very short memory to forget the bad ones.

MAC O'GRADY

These greens are so fast I have to hold my putter over the ball and hit it with the shadow.

SAM SNEAD

The income tax has made more liars out of the American people than golf has.

WILL ROGERS

If I swung a gavel the way I swung that golf club, the nation would be in a helluva mess.

TIP O'NEILL

Titleist has offered me a big contract not to play its balls.

BOB HOPE

A good golf course is like good music. It does not necessarily appeal the first time one plays it.

ALISTER MACKENZIE

Golf is like love. One day
you think you are too old, and
the next day you want to
do it again.

ROBERTO DE VICENZO

Give me golf clubs, the fresh
air, and a beautiful partner, and
you can keep my golf clubs
and the fresh air.

JACK BENNY

Anything I want it to be. For instance, the hole right here is a par 47, and yesterday I birdied the sucker.

WILLIE NELSON

(when asked what was par on a Texas golf course he owns)

However unlucky you may be, it really is not fair to expect your adversary's grief for your undeserved misfortunes to be as poignant as your own.

HORACE HUTCHINSON

If they [southern people] know you are working at home, they think nothing of walking right in for coffee. But they wouldn't dream of interrupting you at golf.

HARPER LEE

I received as much joy from coaxing a first-time pupil, a woman from Paris, into hitting the ball into the air so that she could go back to France and play golf with her husband as I did from watching the development of all the fine players I have been lucky enough to know.

HARVEY PENICK

He plays the game of golf as if he has a plane to catch. As if he were double-parked and left the meter running. Guys move slower leaving hotel fires.

JIM MURRAY

(on Corey Pavin)

To get an elementary grasp of the game of golf, a human must learn, by endless practice, a continuous and subtle series of highly unnatural movements, involving about sixty-four muscles, that result in a seemingly natural swing, taking all of two seconds to begin and end.

ALISTAIR COOKE

I have a bad attitude right now. And that's much worse than a bad golf swing.

PAYNE STEWART

(on his performance at the

1994 Masters)

At Jinja there is both hotel and golf course. The latter is, I believe, the only course in the world which posts a special rule that the player may remove his ball from hippopotamus footprints.

EVELYN WAUGH

There is one categorical imperative, "Hit the Ball," but there are no minor absolutes.

SIR WALTER SIMPSON

I was three over: one over a house, one over a patio, and one over a swimming pool.

GEORGE BRETT

And the wind shall say:
"Here were decent godless
people:
Their only monument the
asphalt road
And a thousand lost golf balls."

T. S. ELIOT

I'm working as hard as I can to get my life and my cash to run out at the same time. If I can just die after lunch Tuesday, everything will be perfect.

DOUG SANDERS

Let's face it, 95 percent of this game is mental. A guy plays lousy golf, he doesn't need a pro, he needs a shrink.

TOM MURPHY

Arnold has more people watching him park the car than we do out on the course.

LEE TREVINO

(on Arnold Palmer)

A game in which you claim
the privileges of age, and retain
the playthings of childhood.

SAMUEL JOHNSON

I didn't hit any spectators. I did get one bass, though.

FUZZY ZOELLER

(on hitting the ball into a lake)

One of the remarkable things about Walter Hagen was the fact that, even in their defeat, his opponents all had tremendous affection for him.

FRED CORCORAN

I'll shoot my age if I have to live to be 105.

BOB HOPE

Excessive golfing dwarfs the intellect. Nor is this to be wondered at when we consider that the more fatuously vacant the mind is, the better for play. It has been observed that absolute idiots play the steadiest.

SIR WALTER SIMPSON

Be funny on a golf course?
Do I kid my best friend's
mother about her heart
condition?

PHIL SILVERS

I don't want that thing in my hand if lightning hits. The Man up there knows I've been a bad boy.

LEE TREVINO

(after throwing his club to the ground during a thunderstorm)

Shall the married man play golf? This admits of no argument. Certainly. Of all the plagues to a woman in the house is a man during the day.

DR. PROUDFOOT

If you three-putt the first green, they'll never remember it. But if you three-putt the eighteenth, they'll never forget it.

WALTER HAGEN

The nice thing about these [golf] books is that they usually cancel each other out. One book tells you to keep your eye on the ball; the next says not to bother. Personally, in the crowd I play with, a better idea is to keep your eye on your partner.

JIM MURRAY

Some people say I play erratic golf. What they mean is I frequently play lousy.

TOM SHAW

If Charles II felt in any way
troubled he was at least allowed
to have recourse to the
distractions of golf.

SAMUEL R. GARDNER

Shoot a lower score than everybody else.

BEN HOGAN

(on the secret of winning the U.S. Open)

If you pick up a golfer and hold it close to your ear, like a conch shell, and listen, you will hear an alibi.

FRED BECK

Dan would rather play golf than have sex any day.

MARILYN QUAYLE

Golf is 20 percent mechanics and technique. The other 80 percent is philosophy, humor, tragedy, romance, melodrama, companionship, camaraderie, cussedness, and conversation.

GRANTLAND RICE

My swing is so bad I look like a caveman killing his lunch.

LEE TREVINO

The fairways were so narrow you had to walk down them single file.

SAM SNEAD

The least thing upset him on the links. He missed short putts because of the uproar of butterflies in the adjoining meadows.

P. G. WODEHOUSE

If a man is to get into a hazard let it be a bad one. Let the lies within your hazard be as bad as you please—the worse the better. So leave your whins without any pruning or thinning and if the bottom of your sand bunker gets smooth-beaten, howk it up.

HORACE HUTCHINSON

Golf is tougher than my first wife.

KEN GREEN

There are two things the players on tours should realize: Adults will copy your swing, and young people will follow your example.

HARVEY PENICK

I don't play golf to feel bad. I play bad golf and still feel good.

LESLIE NIELSEN

St. Andrews? I feel like
I'm back visiting an old
grandmother. She's crotchety
and eccentric but also elegant.
Anyone who doesn't fall in love
with her has no imagination.

TONY LEMA

I remember he was so wild that when the word got out that he was taking a lesson, the parking lot was emptied of Cadillacs in five minutes.

MAX ELBIN

(on President Richard Nixon)

The poetic temperament is the worst for golf. It dreams of brilliant drives, iron shots laid dead, and long putts holed, while in real golf success waits for him who takes care of the fozzles and leaves the fine shots to take care of themselves.

SIR WALTER SIMPSON

If a lot of people gripped a knife and fork the way they do a golf club, they'd starve to death.

SAM SNEAD

Golf is a science, the study of a lifetime, in which you can exhaust yourself but never your subject.

DAVID FORGAN

Playing in the U.S. Open is like tippy-toeing through hell.

JERRY McGEE

The score a player reports on any hole should always be regarded as his opening offer.

THOMAS MULLIGAN

All I can do is start it. The Lord handles it from there.

JIMMY DEMARET

(on putting)

I think I fail a bit less than everyone else.

JACK NICKLAUS

I played as much golf as I could in North Dakota, but summer up there is pretty short. It usually falls on Tuesday.

MIKE MORLEY

(on being from North Dakota)

We tournament golfers are
much overrated. We get paid
too much.

TOM WATSON

My golf game reminds me of Woody Hayes's football game—three yards and a cloud of dust.

BILL DOOLEY

Never bet with a man named "One-Iron."

TOM SHARP

I don't play well enough to be allowed to throw my clubs.

LOU HOLTZ

You get to know more of the character of a man in a round of golf than in six months of political experience.

LLOYD GEORGE

I miss the putt. I miss the putt. I miss the putt. I make.

SEVE BALLESTEROS

(explaining his four-putt on the sixteenth green at the 1986 Masters)

Keep on hitting it straight
until the wee ball goes in
the hole.

JAMES BRAID

It's nice to look down the fairway and see your mother on the left and your father on the right. You know that no matter whether you hook it or slice it, somebody is going to be there to kick it back in the fairway.

LARRY NELSON

The game required a certain cold toughness of mind, and absorption of will. There was not an athlete I talked to from other sports who did not hold the professional golfer in complete awe, with thanksgiving that golf was not their profession.

GEORGE PLIMPTON

There is nothing natural
about the golf swing.

BEN HOGAN

(after being complimented on his

natural swing)

The more I practice, the luckier I get.

GARY PLAYER

If you think it's hard to meet new people, try picking up the wrong golf ball.

JACK LEMMON

Yes, you're probably right about the left hand, but the fact is that I take my check with the right hand.

BOBBY LOCKE

(responding to critics of his left-handed grip)

Golf is a game in which you yell fore, shoot six, and write down five.

PAUL HARVEY

Playing golf is like chasing a quinine pill around a cow pasture.

WINSTON CHURCHILL

They call it golf because all of the other four-letter words were taken.

RAYMOND FLOYD

Don't hit things you aren't supposed to. An important aspect of golf is knowing what to hit.

P. J. O'ROURKE

One of the advantages bowling has over golf is that you seldom lose a bowling ball.

DON CARTER

It is a test of temper, a trial of honor, a revealer of character. It means going into God's out of doors, getting close to nature, fresh air, and exercise, a sweeping of mental cobwebs and a genuine relaxation of tired tissues

DAVID FORGAN

A lot more people beat me now.

DWIGHT EISENHOWER

(on his game after the presidency)

The only thing of real value
that you can take from the
driving range to the first tee is
a pocketful of range balls.

THOMAS MULLIGAN

I could only hit balls thrown down at my feet.

TOM WATSON

(when asked why he didn't pursue a baseball career)

Golf has probably kept
more people sane than
psychiatrists have.

HARVEY PENICK

Hold up a 1-iron and walk.
Even God can't hit a 1-iron.

LEE TREVINO

(on how to avoid being struck

by lightning)

Like life, golf can be humbling. However, little good comes from brooding about mistakes we've made. The next shot, in golf or in life, is the big one.

GRANTLAND RICE

Ninety percent of the putts that fall short don't go in.

Yogi Berra

Being left-handed is a big advantage: no one knows enough about your swing to mess you up with advice.

BOB CHARLES

I'd rather be on a golf course than eat. If I couldn't go and dig some dirt, you might as well put me in a box.

PETE DYE

I'd like to see the fairways more narrow. Then everybody would have to play from the rough, not just me.

SEVE BALLESTEROS

I like golf because I can go out and hit a little white ball that doesn't move and doesn't hit back. It should be easy, but it isn't.

LAWRENCE TAYLOR

I don't trust doctors. They are like golfers. Every one has a different answer to your problem.

SEVE BALLESTEROS

Golf is the most fun you can have without taking your clothes off.

CHI CHI RODRIGUEZ

Let the club swing itself through. Help it on all you can but do not you begin to hit with it. Let it do its work itself and it will do it well. Interfere with it, and it will be quite adequately revenged.

HORACE HUTCHINSON

If it really made sense to "let the club do the work," you'd just say, "Driver, wedge to the green, one-putt," and walk to the next tee.

THOMAS MULLIGAN

In golf, when we hit a foul ball, we've got to go out and play it.

SAM SNEAD

(comparing golf to baseball)

If you call on God to improve the results of a shot while it is still in motion, you are using "an outside agency" and subject to appropriate penalties under the rules of golf.

HENRY LONGHURST

First, hitting the ball. Second, finding out where it went.

TOM WATSON

(commenting on how he would help President Ford's golf game)

A round of golf requires no more than three hours, fifteen minutes. If you are on the course longer than this, a marshal will come escort you off.

SIGN ON FIRST TEE AT
COURSE IN SCOTLAND

Golf is the only sport that a professional can enjoy playing with his friends. Can Larry Holmes enjoy fighting one of his friends?

CHI CHI RODRIGUEZ

Unlike the other Scotch game of whiskey drinking, excess in it is not injurious to the health.

SIR WALTER SIMPSON

I play with friends
sometimes, but there are
never friendly games.

BEN HOGAN

Dividing the swing into its parts is like dissecting a cat. You'll have blood and guts and bones all over the place. But you won't have a cat.

ERNEST JONES

Through years of experience I have found that air offers less resistance than dirt.

JACK NICKLAUS

(after teeing a golf ball exceedingly high)

Of all the thousands of swing-training aids and gimmicks I have seen, the best is one you can buy at the hardware store if you don't already have it in your garage or toolshed.

It is the common weed cutter.

HARVEY PENICK

The suit is so stiff. I can't do
this with two hands but I'm
going to try a little sand
trap shot here.

ALAN SHEPARD,
ASTRONAUT

(golfing on the surface of the moon)

All I've got against golf is it takes you so far from the clubhouse.

ERIC LINKLATER

If you watch a game, it's fun. If you play it, it's recreation. If you work at it, it's golf.

BOB HOPE

Golfers play golf to prove that they can mentally overcome the pressures that golf puts upon them. The fact that if they didn't play golf at all they would not have to endure or overcome its pressures may not occur to them.

PETER GAMMOND

I've never had a coach in my life. When I find one who can beat me, then I'll listen.

LEE TREVINO

I've quit drinking. But don't tell anybody. I don't want to ruin my image.

RAYMOND FLOYD

The British Open probably would have died if the American stars hadn't started going over to play in it more regularly the last fifteen years. Arnold Palmer saved it, but as far as I'm concerned he didn't do us any favors.

DAVE HILL

Years ago we discovered the exact point, the dead center of middle age. It occurs when you are too young to take up golf and too old to rush to the net.

FRANKLIN ADAMS

A golf course may be said to have to satisfy four definite requirements. It must supply the opportunity for the pleasure of practicing an athletic art, entail the necessity of providing an adequate test of skill, demand mental agility, and, lastly, a disciplinary scheme by which the virtuous cannot be rewarded without a penalty being inflicted on the sinner.

PETER LAWLESS

363

Golf is not just an exercise;
it's an adventure, a romance . . .
a Shakespeare play in which
disaster and comedy are
intertwined.

HAROLD SEGALL

If you can smile when all around you have lost their heads—you must be the caddy.

ANONYMOUS

You know you're on the
Senior Tour when your back
goes out more than you do.

BOB BRUCE

Golf combines two favorite
American pastimes: taking long
walks and hitting things
with a stick.

P. J. O'ROURKE

If your adversary is badly bunkered, there is no rule against your standing over him and counting his strokes aloud, with increasing gusto as their number mounts up; but it will be a wise precaution to arm yourself with the niblick before doing so, so as to meet him on equal terms.

HORACE HUTCHINSON

How can they beat me?
I've been struck by lightning,
had two back operations, and
been divorced twice.

LEE TREVINO

*(on his chances for taking the title
at the 1983 British Open)*

369

The older you get, the easier it is to shoot your age.

JERRY BARBER

Never give a golfer an ultimatum unless you're prepared to lose.

ABIGAIL VAN BUREN

("Dear Abby")

Golf has drawbacks.
It is possible, by too much of it,
to destroy the mind.

SIR WALTER SIMPSON

Golf appeals to the idiot in us and the child. What child does not grasp the pleasure principle of miniature golf? Just how childlike golf players become is proven by their frequent inability to count past five.

JOHN UPDIKE

●

THE TEXT OF THIS BOOK

WAS SET IN COCHIN

AND COOPER BLACK

BY SALLY McELWAIN.

BOOK DESIGN BY

JUDITH STAGNITTO ABBATE